AF570744

ACE

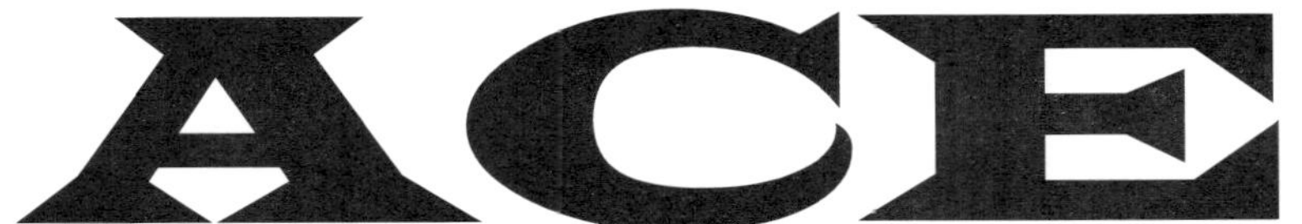

ACE

Richard Carr

Winner of the
2008 Washington Prize

THE WORD WORKS
WASHINGTON, D.C.

First Edition First Printing
Ace

The WORD WORKS
PO Box 42164
Washington, DC 20015
editor@wordworksdc.com

Cover art: Oosoom at Wikipedia

Book design, typography by Janice Olson

Printed by Signature Book Printing, Inc.
www.sbpbooks.com

Library of Congress Number: 2008935238

International Standard Book Number: 9780915380701

CONTENTS

I: ACE

II: CAROL

III: MISS PRINCESS

IV: LITTLE ACE

I:

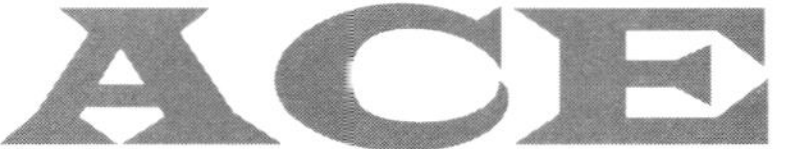

AUTO PARTS

I started my search for him in the salvage yard
in and around the junked cars and vans
somehow all the same color and sprouting the same yellow weed
imagining him already grown into a boy
and playing where I played
climbing the stacked wrecks keenly
for the view across the rail yard and down to the river
though I was not so sentimental
that I would go to a playground looking for my daughter on the
    swings
for of course I knew the girl and knew she was old enough to be in
    a bar
drinking working whatever
whereas I had never met her son
and so thought of him in a state of joy
a grandson among the auto parts.

A SUITABLE CALLING

I would call the boy Ace
after myself
a name I picked up for being awkward as a kid
sideswiping parked cars
twisting up my bicycle in crashes
a sarcasm
a jeer
hey Ace nice flying
but a title I later polished clean
running errands for the local dealers
never failing to deliver find or find out
so that it became my logo
my business card
though maybe not a suitable calling for the boy.

GROUPIE FREAKY

My old lady was cherry
straight blond short shorts groupie freaky
who called me across the river for some wild dancing
her act
and kept me coming back until we got married
for about nine hours
after which she had our kid Miss Princess
and graduated to bartending
which is when I lost interest in her career
though I kept tabs on her for a long time from a distance
until recently when I heard she died
Carol her name was Carol died
of cancer AIDS suicide bones breasts killers killers
OD probably.

VAGABONDING

Miss Princess learned vagabonding from her mother
and ran away without graduating from school
as we all did in various states of combustion
the girl in particular setting fire to bridges
her mother's apartment
her boyfriend's hair
someone's car
in order to make her pregnancy pure
all her own
and all alone she would have her baby and raise him better than
    whoever
never pausing to wonder who would help her in all this anyway
maybe no one
and therefore I wanted to see the boy who as a consequence of his
    hardship
would be magnificent.

SEED OF FIRE

I imagined my grandson growing brilliantly
a seed of fire sizzling and sparking loudly
becoming Little Ace
by falling face first onto the sidewalk
and getting up each time another year older
still crying maybe but starting to scar over
while behind the white tissue his first primitive plan took shape
to run away and handle things on his own
appreciating early his destiny
that he would siphon from the gas tank of life
unaware of my poor example and long days on the street
though it is possible he has seen me at the roadside
when I lift the hood of my car
to examine the silence.

MOVE IT

I'm looking for a better car
no a superlative ride
a low coupe of classic Detroit
old sheet metal
and a new leather jacket
black and no more boyish night terrors
nasty crawlies in the seat cushions
for I am hardtop ironclad crash-tested
and only need someplace safe to sleep
or sleep it off
or sit up sleepless
enough car to cover my head when it snows
and move me down the road
when the cop says move it.

AGAINST RATTLING

I'll teach the boy to drive recklessly
a glint in his eye
to guide him
a can of beer between his legs
to test him
his free hand gripping the wheel
a cigarette pinched in his fist
a gleam in his eye for speed
a curve in the road to hold his focus
against rattling knees
his free hand on the radio dial
his free hand raking back his hair
a tear in his eye on the straightaway
the wind in his eye for the getaway.

FRIENDLY BEERS

I spend my days in bars and only bars
searching for Miss Princess in her element
bars down by the river my old haunts mostly razed
bars downtown that still rock
bars in the suburbs with bowling lanes chicken wings mall access
Vegas?
she's no whore
is she?
no I still hope to find her in a corner bar
a smoky pool table jukebox joint
a fading generation of old men and foggy old witches
drinking friendly beers called Bud Miller Mick
like guys you know
in the weedy peeling clapboard neighborhoods of home.

SIX-PACK

Driving around the cemetery with a six-pack carelessly
I can't find her grave
Carol's to ask her advice in all this
none too bright though she was
she was smart about her kid
and daisies and tree bark and crystal gems and whatnot
claiming traces of celestial matter
had passed through her body
some lodging and working its way to her fingertips
so that her touch could heal
maybe did heal me once
and wanting to believe in her again
I stop at a freshly filled hole sprinkled with grass seed
and try to think deep.

ALLEY WARY

I see Little Ace fighting in the war
driving his humvee into a fight
which might never end but spread
street to street
country to country and into all minds
and into the dreams of little boys certain they will die
in a fight
better that he hide himself
walk down the alley wary
step wide of the overturned dumpster and the dark door
put an end to curiosity
the rustling in a pile of trash bags and greasy boxes
a danger now
better that he hide from me.

BULLET

The view from the glass elevator rising twenty-eight stories
does not help my search
the city all detours
emergency vehicles struggling for life in blocked traffic
my heart on fire
a black blaze of burning plastic prescription unfilled
the glossy capsule
sliding down the side of the building in a slow dissolve
my prayer
a worm wriggling through scripture
the elevated expressway of apocalypse and redemption
collapsing in a quake rattling my vision
a bullet of pain in my chest
as I topple in the lobby in a blur of failure.

BETTER POVERTY

Damn that girl
the little hothead runaway delinquent
never lifting her face in daylight
surely a liar a tough a grubber
a car too unreliable for the road
the tires too bald the smoke too blue
I should know
but if she must ride low
I could wish her at least a better poverty
give her an apron and basket like an old time peasant
religious potions to keep her well
a wooden cradle
her mother
to help.

SMALL STURDY

I carry a pristine hundred in my rancid wallet
to show the boy
proving what
in my mind
I buy him a small sturdy bicycle
and follow him around the block in my car
observing him
peddling hard like he has to get somewhere
head down
elbows flung wide
until he skids to a halt in a treeless grassless yard
looks up at me
his hair a parched tuft
nothing impresses him.

GONE DRY

I want to miss her
Carol and her green touch
and cruising the alley behind our old building
I sometimes stop to shake the dusty mustard weeds
encroaching on the chain link gate
or go in and sit on the back stoop
among the little creepers dandling in the cracks like curly hair
wonder maybe if the morning glories climbing the creosote utility pole
are hers
if her pots of basil and tomatoes on the roof
are gone
almost all the green gone dry and silent outside
but not inside
where it is raining and Carol is abundant.

DENTED HULK

For a hundred I got a used utility van
a dented hulk practically derelict
but enough
for keeping things locked up
and for sleep
in the windowless mute interior
just enough
whipping the engine until it screams
for chugging down the industrial boulevard
to the big river where the trains and barges exchange loads
my boxy vehicle like a small cargo container blending in
or like a sarcophagus
waiting to be pried open one day
by a strong young man in leather gloves.

II:

CAROL

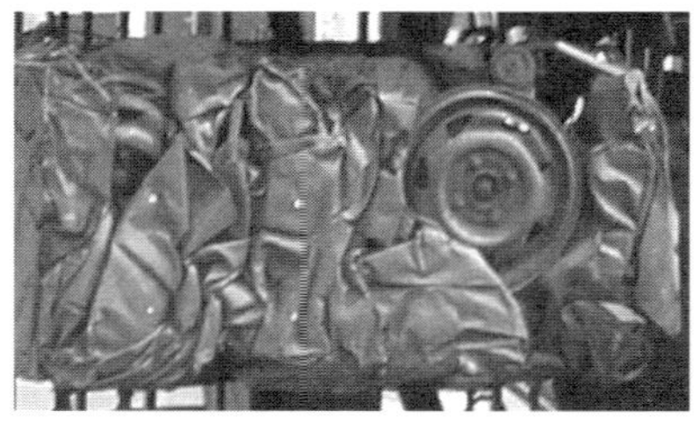

SWEPT UP

The first thing I remember is waking after the accident
my spirit swept up on a swift wind pouring
through the shattered windshield
a cool stream flowing across my bloody face
rushing through the back window and out over the trunk and up
up
into the night and I was flying
and I had always wanted to fly at night
and I looked back
down through the bare trees
at all the helpful determined anxious people surrounding the car
and wished them luck
as they dwindled into the fog
and then I was free.

COCKY

I should be angry
letting that scrawny Ace get me pregnant
his hair beautiful jet black long like a rock 'n' roller
he always sat at the back bar in the dark
left me alone on stage
played pool nonchalant funny and a little mean
made guys mad
but no one touched him because of his drug connections
or maybe his reputation in a fight
little-man syndrome and all that
though really it was his cocky style that kept him out of trouble
and attracted me to him
to hell with it if he never left a tip
watching me from the back bar all alone.

FULL-BLOWN

The peonies shouldering the front steps
first attract ants
shrewd ants climbing the stems
to the syrupy big buds ready to bloom
explode
and then they do and that's it
they bloom in great heaps of heavy color
one mound a dark engorged pink
the other billowing white
all dotted with wet yellow
but then tomorrow the petals decay and detach
and scatter on the ground like kitchen garbage
and now you have to love them
with full-blown love.

AMONG THE STARS

I want to hold a baby again
feel the squeeze of little fingers
on my one big one
look into the eyes
which in a child are like stone calendars
predicting comets
and the eclipses of the new life
the murmuring gurgling voice hoo hoo
recalling tundra swans passing over at night
a living constellation
as from a witch's fire fed with herbs
sparks rise in startled flocks
returning to their element among the stars
my arm outstretched.

HEARTS AND THORNS

Sometimes I wonder about my daughter
where she is
who is she with
does she need money
is she still using
does she still have that knotty hair
has she gotten more tattoos
those hearts and thorns and drops of blood
has she torn her clothes
does she eat
did she grow deep
in her pregnancy
has she grown beautiful
in motherhood.

COOL DOWN

True that I am freaky
certainly in the early years burned some brain cells
on recreational drugs
alright heavy drugs
then lived on White Russians
to cool down
then tea and cream to warm up
and dry out
and everything always contaminated by cigarettes
coating my hair with sticky nicotine
thickening and peppering my complexion
lowering my voice
until one day someone called me a skank
or maybe no one but I believed it.

GOLDEN POLLEN

Sitting in meditation with upturned hands
calming the commotions of the mind
all the fuss
I forget where I am
all my faults
time passing in darkness behind my blood-crusted eyes
feels fresh like breathing cool air
exhaling it fully
cleansing my whole body
until nothing is left but shimmering particles in space
which blow away with the next breath
so that I am nothing now
but a few granules of golden pollen
sailing on a solar wind.

TALK-SHOW QUEEN

My beautiful girl was a victim
of her own savage independence
teenage cunning
shameless devices
extravagant desires
all braided into the brutal stupidity of her age
she saw no choice but to run away
walk out of the kitchen while I talked
explaining all the facts about her needs and interests
covering all the fascinating info
dispensing advice like a talk-show queen
suddenly canceled
and what did she really want in her weedy heart
but a better mother.

HARD YEARS

Knowing he was always watching me during the hard years
I turned up my nose at Ace
though I caught him
and sometimes kept him in the corner of my eye
as he stared at me over his sunglasses
from behind the wheel of his car parked half a block down
or sometimes
I lingered in front of my building
back turned
and I don't know why
I posed like an arrogant mannequin and waited
until I heard him pull into the street
muscle a U-turn
and roll away.

OUR KIND

My daughter's baby is no angel I'm sure
but crouching and wary
cradle-mute
his heavy-lidded eyes dark with disturbed intelligence
what would he know about our happiness
he would steal our grief
and make a ticklish giggling boy of it
a deranged solace
for a family without arms or feet
lynched in a tree
buried face down
the child left to undo his own buttons
pull off his shoes
for which we love him as one of our kind.

DOING MOVES

I taught my daughter to dance
gave her a stage name
for fun
bought her a denim skirt and tiny T
so cute
and after that the good days came
picking songs and doing moves
falling on the couch together
relaxing with magazines
makeup
hair
like friends
and so we lived happily in the night
after my shift.

FERNS

I lived alone with ferns in every room
therefore planning a suicide
was more curiosity about the afterlife
the gateways and intriguing possibilities
than severing pain from its root
and so I played make-believe death
made imaginary mourners
friends who would celebrate my passing
into a world of flowering meadows
and fulfilling knowledge
not foreseeing the terrible blindness of the grave
thinking fondly it would end the excruciations of a life
lived alone among ferns
hung everywhere for health and serenity.

DARK THORN

Imagining my baby grandson
milk and sweet cereal in the morning
a day of toys and TV
kills me
losing my daughter's hand
momentarily in a crowd at the mall
misplacing her again and again
and one day finding only a hair on her pillow
kills me
and losing Ace
who loved me first and last in the world
whom I still imagine intimately in the night
coming to me with his dark thorn
kills me.

COCKTAIL-STICKY

When I'm too tired to bartend another hour
too ugly anymore to get tips
too distracted to mix drinks right
my feet two bricks clomping on cobblestones
my neck a battering ram
when I am white blouse and black vest
uniformed and cocktail-sticky
the monkey of tourists
donkey of locals
reduced to a despicable little smile
of bad teeth
when I am a quick cigarette in the alley
I remember with listless satisfaction
that I am dead.

BLACKBIRDS

I wanted to get closer to them
and drove close to the edge of the road
to better see the wildflowers cattails redwing blackbirds
expressway wildlife
thriving in the drainage ditch
unreachable
still I stared impolitely
away from my human neighbors on the highway
starkly into the mushy green preserve
jerked back by honks
but always returning to the thing I could not have
could not love
without merging myself with it
and spontaneously swerved into my exit.

III:

MISS PRINCESS

THUNDERCLOUD

Mother clung to me with bird-like claws
always on my shoulder
plucking at my ear
whenever she perceived a danger
a crack in the sidewalk
a thundercloud
a boy
until my ear bled
and I filled it with piercings
against her relentless chirping
used clatter and jangle of bracelets and chains
against her touch
and constant music rippling through my hair
against the sight of her.

LURKER

I heard Ace is looking for me
on the wrong side of town
good
because my father is nobody
a lizard
says nothing in the sun
the lurker
hurt my mother too much with his spying
a stalker on our street
sniffing nosy
like a mean dog in the alley
a wet rat on the fence
a slick drug-rat in his black car
and never brought money.

OUT TO LIVE

Raising my own child would prove
I'm mature
so I wasn't running away from home or anything
or someone
but looking for space freedom the true me
because who needs a stupid boyfriend
or stupid anyone else
so I packed my jeans skirts tops boots tights and one lace glove
acne stuff hair stuff makeup toothbrush aspirin
chips maple syrup popcorn bananas napkins
and set out to live in the park
then looked back
and took my mom's tip jar
to get a good start.

FLASH

I gave a bum a handjob for twenty dollars
but he didn't have twenty dollars
so I kicked him until his face puffed up
but really I was kicking myself
another time I ate toothpaste
then I checked out books from the library
and sold them but no one bought any
so I dumped them in the subway
for someone else to read
and one day in a flash
I grabbed a designer handbag from a street vendor
not real designer but better than my school backpack
and I could use it to lift items from the goodwill store
but not department stores they chase you.

SQUEEZED

On instinct I walked into the brightest place
its marquee blinking even in the day
a club called Broadway Lights
which sounded promising
like the real thing
and said I have experience
lying to the cute bar manager
easily
pretending to be my mother
but no I don't dance I lied less comfortably
noticing the blackened windows
the stage the pole the booths
but I want to work
and squeezed his knee truthfully.

UNDER BRIDGES

A girl can't have a baby alone
what was I thinking
better to go home
except life was better at the bar
because at the bar I was tough and cool
and I wore whatever I wanted
all black
and made my own money
felt like a lot
washing glasses stocking liquor hefting cases of beer
and mopping after closing
the last one to go home at night
which is how I like it
walking under bridges awnings plane-trees streetlamps careless.

YELLOW SHADE

Some days I wanted to go home bad
cried for my bed and my pillows
my posters and trophies
unicorns
my magic wand with a star on the end
but who was listening
no one
except maybe someone in the next apartment
but no one ever saw inside my little room
the dresser leaning against the bed
or ever knocked on the door
bedside lamp with a yellow shade
or stood in the street looking up
searching left and right for my window.

MIRACULOUS

I pretended during the years of my new life
that I had no history
no wars no climate no people
at first darkly like a heartbroken nun
cherishing her sins
then out in the open like a witch
unafraid of dirty looks
or fire
pronouncing outrageous judgment on any and everything
but her own buried secret
always acting
as if I had sprung from a crack in the sidewalk
fully formed scarred snow-capped
miraculous me.

DREADED SEEING

I missed both my parents
eventually
the real one
I looked for in tarot cards
sure I would meet her eyes there
but I obsessed on the secretive one
dreaded seeing him somewhere
sitting bolt upright in the back of a slow-moving cab
or down the street shoving a newspaper into a trash basket
or right beside me
leaning in a doorway smoking
and in creepy dreams he brought me incredible gifts
a couch a computer a new car
and I hated myself for accepting them while my mother watched.

BROKEN GLASS REMAINS

Bartending downtown at the Sky Room
when my mother died in a ditch
I quit my job on the spot
didn't cry at first I was so angry
but took a long walk up Broadway
walked in the park
tried to walk backward through my life
went looking for my old boyfriend
at the broken glass remains of our high school
as though
as if to give back to him
nothing
found Mom's apartment building with its ivy
and flower boxes as always.

HOME NOW

On uneven nights
I push one leg out of my burrow of blankets
and lower the foot to the floor
with effort
shuffle to the bathroom for a pill
bend to sip from the tap
a bent cornstalk in a flowerpot
crisp husk
I light a cigarette
and drop it in the toilet with the others
the blackening dead of a wrecked ship
floating mutely at two three four a.m.
my shift passing without me
the bar my only home now.

DRINKERS

I miss the bright expectant eyes of drinkers
shedding glints of happiness onto the bar-top
and the bruised eyes of drinkers
swollen and sweet as plums
and eyes deep in street debt
cut by razor blades
or holy eyes bathed in blue neon
and devil eyes made of ice cubes
boiling in their sockets
or strangled and weedy aquarium eyes
with clouds of green light
or no light only green slime
and eyes dripping cactus milk
thorny stinging eyes like mine.

SOFT SHOES

I'll go back to bartending
never marry
own only soft shoes
maybe get a cat
two cats
read romance novels detective novels
make cookies on Saturday
cut my own hair
save for a trip to Paris
or Las Vegas
start dancing again
at home
I'm so fat
it's all I know.

STICK-FIGURE

A small stick-figure of girlhood in me
still wants her Daddy
his touch
the rough texture of his thumb on my cheek
the feel of his scuffed biker boots
thick indigo denim
the little knobs of his knees
which I clutched
standing up to him
holding up the weight of his hand on my head
as he stood to go
leaving a pencil sketch of himself
for me to erase
and brush away.

SIDE DOOR

A girl cuts her arms
burns letters
runs in all directions trying to pull it all together
pulling it all apart
as uncertain about her hair as her homework
and yet with the scavenged confidence of a runaway
the rigid poise
the high-wire realism
I thought I was right about everything
I was sure about my mother
knew all about my father and everything about boys
and in time I felt a shivering certainty about my pregnancy
and went quickly to the side door clinic
to end it.

IV:

LITTLE ACE

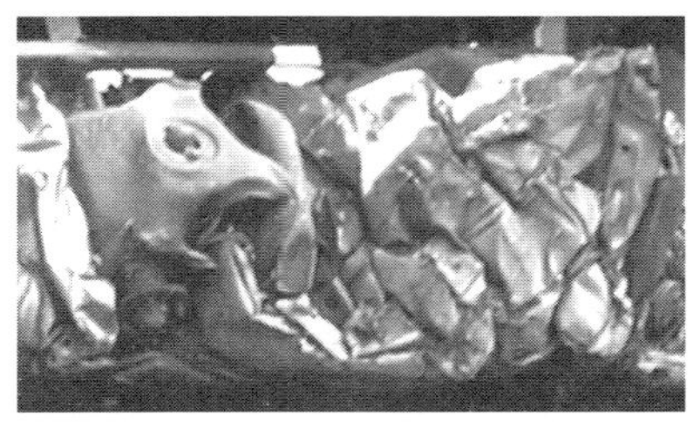

CHAMPAGNE

I live in a flowering meadow
there is so little for me to understand
I have tiny hands tiny feet
perfect toes the size of champagne bubbles
a wisp of spinal cord
like a candle wick in soft wax
gently shut eyes
heartbeat
heartbeat
a flowering meadow for me to understand
I kick and grasp
I suck my thumb
there is so little for me
except this my great beginning.

ANGEL

I float on a cloud above the world
not an angel
but more like the cloud itself
chaotic and serene
I am here
a broken relationship of atoms and energies
like fallen leaves
coalescing in a swirl of wind
I persist
an echo of my existence pitched icily high
my cry both familiar and uncanny
a baby no more
yet I cling to being
and suckle from its source.

WAR OF PINPRICKS

I go down in the January night
the cold does not touch me
and visit my grandfather in his car
not to aid him
but to spy on his dreams
watch him grasp at the air with limp hands
snatching breaths
his body still believing in a waking world
supplied by shocks
intruders bee-stings snapshots
shattered glass and fresh snow sprinkled on the dashboard
each night a war of pinpricks fought hopelessly
until he is startled awake
how he must love life.

CRAYON FIGURES

The tendrils of me have spread
reaching into the ten thousand lives of my ancestors
libraries of consciousness
perched like fortifications on desert hilltops
for me to explore
though I absorb only dust
preternatural boy conditional spirit
fated to a demonic physicality in the world
red crayon bombs falling on blue crayon figures
the graffiti of a child
language
but not voice
I am unhappy
and stir lazily in the dust.

BEAUTIFUL WITHOUT ME

I hardly knew my mother
but I see she has grown beautiful without me
and terrible in her secret heart
humming a tune off-key
as she brushes her cropped hair
pointlessly
unless it is to look in the mirror
and into the dark room behind her
to some unclear past or future
time halted
preserving in her a delicate state of nausea
her eyebrows drawn together angrily
at gunpoint
nothing is demanded of her.

HOWEVER DARING

I don't care about my father
however charming
however daring diligent dusty
athlete addict I don't care
bleacher boy
backseat boy
teenage boy ignorant of all but fucking
and ignorant of that too
what use are chromosomes
hair color eye color the spray-painted lockers of flesh
to a ghost
what use is a father without arms feet face
who was never viable
but cut and scraped out of memory.

COMET

I can never be any closer to my grandmother
than I am now
for she is inward
and I am pure emanation
she is a quiet bath
candles and incense
and I am droplets flung from a girl's hair in the rain
I am the fragrance of a thousand peonies
and she is dead
buried under experience her memories all the years
shoveled down onto her while I
escaped
she the deep gravitational embrace
I a tiny comet.

DEMON

The old man's demon
he mine
I would not exist without Ace
my progenitor and energy source
prime mover
when he throws the football I run to catch it
so too he would cease to move forward
without my calling
like the rustling of a rat in the alley
drawing a dog into the garbage
he's curious
looming
and I am not afraid to meet him
who would not exist without me.

STREET KID

Bound to fight the wars of other men
who see a street kid without a good school
skipping school
and feel he can accomplish their great purpose
men who see a boy riding a bicycle
and believe he brings victory
I arm for the grieving lonely combat of old men
and salute their mysterious cause
without understanding my objective
or comprehending their fear
because I want to help Ace
whom I love
though I don't know what he's looking for
or why he believes in me.

LINGERING

Following the trail of my grandmother's last thoughts
through the fog and debris of lingering possibility
a junkyard of spiritual remains
the wreckage of billions
I look for a tulip
or a purple crocus pushing through snow
a sign
that the fragments of her have fertilized a small plot
in the landscape of death
where to be an individual is meaningless
the self unsalvageable
which is a comfort to some
though it means there are no flowers on the littered plain
and no one to be found.

MIXING DRINKS

Small enough to curl up and hide inside her wristwatch
I observe my mother at work mixing drinks
I love the clank of glassware
servers calling orders
the din of music
flawless on her feet like a ballroom dancer
she dunks me in the sink
water and bubbles stream across my face
her hands move from bottle to bottle like hummingbirds
decisive and efficient
she does not speak
but I know she grieves
while I bask in heavenly neon
useless to her.

NUDGE

At least I can help old Ace
I know he wants to see me
and I could nudge him along
give him a brain tumor
no too slow
or a heart attack
except he fights it
or I could go down to the river where he parks his van at night
and when he runs the engine against the cold
blow the little puffs of clear exhaust
through a crack in the buckled back doors
and make a painless gas chamber
I'm so lonely
I'll do anything for him.

THROUGH THE WINDSHIELD

Ace wakes after a cold sleep
I stare back at him through the windshield
but he is blinded by the glare of morning
and the confusions of night
he wants a grandson
he wants me to be his little boy
and I've tried to change
I've grown evolved adapted and survived
but I can never live up to his dream
I can't catch a ball or ride a bike
I have no pockets no penknife no pet cricket
I will never learn to drive
I'm not that boy
and he would hate me if he could see me.

THE KITE

I'm afraid of what will happen next
existence a kite
always tugging
and who is not afraid to let it go
for we know what happens
the string recedes to nothingness in an instant
while the kite does not at first understand
then it leaps upward with new energy
and flies with the wind as an equal
until it is gone
all our moments are irretrievable
the sky empty
I did not want to die
not like this.

AMONG THE WEEDS

I want to live
though the dead are piled all around me
stacked like junked cars in the jagged embraces of their kind
and stillness
barges moving on the distant river
a locomotive hums in the rail yard
and in this place of shattered intimacy
I know Ace loves me
I don't know how it is possible
but he has returned
stumping through the dust in his big boots
he's looking for me
he is happy among the weeds and wrecks
he knows I am here!

About the author

RICHARD CARR grew up in Blue Earth, Minnesota, and lives in Minneapolis. A former systems analyst, web designer, and tavern manager, he has taught writing and literature at several universities and community colleges. His other poetry collections are *Street Portraits* (The Backwaters Press), *Honey* (Gival Press, winner of the Gival Press Poetry Award) and *Mister Martini* (University of North Texas Press, winner of the Vassar Miller Prize). His chapbooks include *Butterfly and Nothingness* (Mudlark) and *Letters from North Prospect* (Frank Cat Press, winner of the Frank Cat Press Poetry Chapbook Competition).

About the cover art

"Patrons park their car at their own risk." A car park entance in Heath Mill Lane, Deritend, Birmingham, England. Oosoom at Wikipedia.

About the Washington Prize

Ace is the winner of the 2008 Word Works Washington Prize. Richard Carr's manuscript was selected from among 255 manuscripts submitted by American poets.

FIRST READERS:

Cliff Bernier
Doris Brody
Angelyn Donohue
W. Perry Epes
Colin Flanigan
Erich Hintze
Tod Ibrahim
Mike McDermott
Ann Rayburn
Jill Tunick
Doug Wilkinson

SECOND READERS:

Mark Dawson
Brandon D. Johnson
J.D. Smith

FINAL JUDGES:

Karren L. Alenier
J.H. Beall
Miles David Moore
Steven B. Rogers
Nancy White

About the Word Works

The Word Works, a nonprofit literary organization, publishes contemporary poetry in collectors' editions. Since 1981, the organization has sponsored the Washington Prize, a $1,500 award to an American poet. Monthly, The Word Works presents free literary programs in the Chevy Chase Café Muse series, and each summer, free poetry programs are held at the historic Joaquin Miller Cabin in Washington, DC's Rock Creek Park. Annually, two high school students debut in the Miller Cabin Series as winners of the Jacklyn Potter Young Poets Competition.

Since 1974, Word Works programs have included: "In the Shadow of the Capitol," a symposium and archival project on the African-American intellectual community in segregated Washington, DC; the Gunston Arts Center Poetry Series (Ai, Carolyn Forché, Stanley Kunitz, and others); the Poet-Editor panel discussions at the Bethesda Writer's Center (John Hollander, Maurice English, Anthony Hecht, Josephine Jacobsen, and others); Poet's Jam, a multi-arts program series featuring poetry in performance; a poetry workshop at the Center for Creative Non-Violence (CCNV) shelter; and the Arts Retreat in Tuscany. Master Class workshops, an ongoing program, have featured Agha Shahid Ali, Thomas Lux, and Marilyn Nelson.

In 2009, Word Works will have published 67 titles, including work from such authors as Deirdra Baldwin, J.H. Beall, Christopher Bursk, John Pauker, Edward Weismiller, and Mac Wellman. Currently, The Word Works publishes books and occasional anthologies under three imprints: the Washington Prize, the Hilary Tham Capital Collection, and International Editions.

Past grants have been awarded by the National Endowment for the Arts, National Endowment for the Humanities, DC Commission on the Arts & Humanities, Witter Bynner Foundation, Writer's Center, Bell Atlantic, Batir Foundation, and others, including many generous private patrons.

The Word Works has established an archive of artistic and administrative materials in the Washington Writing Archive housed in the George Washington University Gelman Library.

Please enclose a self-addressed, stamped envelope with all inquiries.

The Word Works PO Box 42164 Washington, DC 20015
editor@wordworksdc.com www.wordworksdc.com

OTHER WORD WORKS BOOKS

Karren L. Alenier, Hilary Tham, Miles David Moore, EDS.,
Winners: A Retrospective of the Washington Prize

* Nathalie F. Anderson, ***Following Fred Astaire***

* Michael Atkinson, ***One Hundred Children Waiting for a Train***

Mel Belin, ***Flesh That Was Chrysalis*** (HTC COLLECTION)

* Carrie Bennett, ***biography of water***

* Peter Blair, ***Last Heat***

Doris Brody, ***Judging the Distance*** (HTC COLLECTION)

Sarah Browning, ***Whiskey in the Garden of Eden*** (HTC COLLECTION)

Christopher Conlon, ***Gilbert and Garbo in Love*** (HTC COLLECTION)

Christopher Conlon, ***Mary Falls*** (HTC COLLECTION)

Donna Denizé, ***Broken Like Job*** (HTC COLLECTION)

Moshe Dor, Barbara Goldberg, Giora Leshem, EDS.,
The Stones Remember

James C. Hopkins, ***Eight Pale Women*** (HTC COLLECTION)

James C. Hopkins & Yoko Danno, ***The Blue Door***
(INTERNATIONAL EDITIONS)

Brandon D. Johnson, ***Love's Skin*** (HTC COLLECTION)

Myong-Hee Kim, ***Crow's Eye View: The Infamy of Lee Sang, Korean Poet*** (INTERNATIONAL EDITIONS)

Vladimir Levchev, ***Black Book of the Endangered Species***
(INTERNATIONAL EDITIONS)

* Richard Lyons, ***Fleur Carnivore***

* Fred Marchant, ***Tipping Point***

Judith McCombs, ***The Habit of Fire*** (HTC COLLECTION)

* Ron Mohring, ***Survivable World***

Miles David Moore, ***The Bears of Paris*** (HTC COLLECTION)

Miles David Moore, ***Rollercoaster*** (HTC COLLECTION)

Kathi Morrison-Taylor, ***By the Nest*** (HTC COLLECTION)

Jacklyn Potter, Dwaine Rieves, Gary Stein, EDS.,
Cabin Fever: Poets at Joaquin Miller's Cabin

* Jay Rogoff, ***The Cutoff***

Robert Sargent, ***Aspects of a Southern Story***

Robert Sargent, ***A Woman from Memphis***

* Prartho Sereno, ***Call from Paris***

* Enid Shomer, ***Stalking the Florida Panther***

* John Surowiecki, ***The Hat City after Men Stopped Wearing Hats***

Maria Terrone, ***The Bodies We Were Loaned*** (HTC COLLECTION)

Hilary Tham, ***Bad Names for Women*** (HTC COLLECTION)

Hilary Tham, ***Counting*** (HTC COLLECTION)

Jonathan Vaile, ***Blue Cowboy*** (HTC COLLECTION)

* Miles Waggener, ***Phoenix Suites***

Rosemary Winslow, ***Green Bodies*** (HTC COLLECTION)

* WASHINGTON PRIZE WINNERS